THIS JOURNAL BELONGS TO:

SOCIAL ACCOUNTS

ACCOUNT MANAGEMENT

FACEBOOK

1
URL
USERNAME:
PASSWORD:

INSTAGRAM

2
URL:
USERNAME:
PASSWORD:

PINTEREST

3
URL:
USERNAME:
PASSWORD:

YOUTUBE

4
URL:
USERNAME:
PASSWORD:

BLOG

5
URL:
USERNAME:
PASSWORD:

LINKEDIN

6
URL:
USERNAME:
PASSWORD:

7
URL:
USERNAME:
PASSWORD:

8
URL:
USERNAME:
PASSWORD:

9
URL:
USERNAME:
PASSWORD:

10
URL:
USERNAME:
PASSWORD:

BUSINESS GOALS

QUARTERLY GOAL BREAKDOWN

QUARTER: △ 1   △ 2   △ 3   △ 4   MONTH BEGINNING:

GOAL:

	ACTION STEPS
MONTH:	

	ACTION POINTS FOR COMPLETION
MONTH:	

	ACTION POINTS FOR COMPLETION
MONTH:	

BUSINESS GOALS

QUARTERLY GOALS & ACTION PLAN

QUARTER 1

QUARTER 2

QUARTER 3

QUARTER 4

TOP GOALS PER CHANNEL/PLATFORM

- [ ] 📷 INSTAGRAM
- [ ] 🐦 TWITTER
- [ ] 📌 PINTEREST
- [ ] **f** FACEBOOK
- [ ] ▶ YOUTUBE
- [ ] 🎮 TWITCH
- [ ] 👻 SNAPCHAT
- [ ] **t** TUMBLR
- [ ] **in** LINKEDIN
- [ ] **B** BLOG
- [ ]

NOTES & IDEAS

TARGET AUDIENCE

TARGET AUDIENCE SNAPSHOT AND MARKET OVERVIEW

TARGET AUDIENCE OVERVIEW

AGE ....

GENDER ....

LOCATION ....

EXPERIENCE LEVEL ....

OCCUPATION ....

EDUCATION ....

AVG MONTHLY INCOME ....

NOTES

COMMONLY USED PLATFORMS ☐ ⃝ ☐ f ☐ ▾ ☐ ℗ ☐ ▸ ☐ ✿ ☐ t ☐ in ☐

OTHER INFORMATION:
....

TOP PRODUCTS SOLD

- ....
- ....
- ....
- ....
- ....

TOP FACEBOOK GROUPS/FORUMS

- ....
- ....
- ....
- ....

TOP MARKET INFLUENCERS

- ....
- ....
- ....
- ....
- ....

TOP AUTHORITY BLOGGERS

- ....
- ....
- ....
- ....

NICHE RESEARCH NOTES

BUSINESS CONTACTS

NAME

COMPANY

PHONE

EMAIL

NAME

COMPANY

PHONE

EMAIL

NAME

COMPANY

PHONE

EMAIL

NAME

COMPANY

PHONE

EMAIL

NAME

COMPANY

PHONE

EMAIL

NAME

COMPANY

PHONE

EMAIL

NAME

COMPANY

PHONE

EMAIL

NAME

COMPANY

PHONE

EMAIL

CONTENT PLANNER

SOCIAL MEDIA CONTENT PLANNER

MONDAY
- f ☐
- 🐦 ☐
- 📷 ☐
- 📌 ☐

TUESDAY
- f ☐
- 🐦 ☐
- 📷 ☐
- 📌 ☐

WEDNESDAY
- f ☐
- 🐦 ☐
- 📷 ☐
- 📌 ☐

THURSDAY
- f ☐
- 🐦 ☐
- 📷 ☐
- 📌 ☐

FRIDAY
- f ☐
- 🐦 ☐
- 📷 ☐
- 📌 ☐

SATURDAY
- f ☐
- 🐦 ☐
- 📷 ☐
- 📌 ☐

SUNDAY
- f ☐
- 🐦 ☐
- 📷 ☐
- 📌 ☐

NOTES & REMINDERS

SOCIAL TASKS

SOCIAL MEDIA TASK TRACKER

ACTION/TASK	MON	TUE	WED	THU	FRI	SAT	SUN

ADVERTISING

PAID ADVERTISING – PLANNER & TRACKER

AD SUBJECT:		PUBLISHED:		DURATION:	
CONTENT:					
☐ TWITTER	☐ INSTAGRAM	☐ PINTEREST	☐ FACEBOOK	☐ OTHER	
BUDGET:	CLICKS:	REACH:	VIEWS:	CTR:	

AD SUBJECT:		PUBLISHED:		DURATION:	
CONTENT:					
☐ TWITTER	☐ INSTAGRAM	☐ PINTEREST	☐ FACEBOOK	☐ OTHER	
BUDGET:	CLICKS:	REACH:	VIEWS:	CTR:	

AD SUBJECT:		PUBLISHED:		DURATION:	
CONTENT:					
☐ TWITTER	☐ INSTAGRAM	☐ PINTEREST	☐ FACEBOOK	☐ OTHER	
BUDGET:	CLICKS:	REACH:	VIEWS:	CTR:	

AD SUBJECT:		PUBLISHED:		DURATION:	
CONTENT:					
☐ TWITTER	☐ INSTAGRAM	☐ PINTEREST	☐ FACEBOOK	☐ OTHER	
BUDGET:	CLICKS:	REACH:	VIEWS:	CTR:	

SOCIAL MEDIA

SOCIAL MEDIA ACCOUNT MANAGEMENT

SOCIAL MEDIA ACCOUNTS	FACEBOOK GROUPS/OUTREACH
FACEBOOK.COM/	
TWITTER: @	
PINTEREST.COM/	
INSTAGRAM.COM/	
YOUTUBE.COM/	

SOCIAL MEDIA NOTES & IDEAS GOING FORWARD

OTHER SOCIAL MEDIA ACCOUNTS

CHANNEL	URL	USERNAME	PASSWORD

SPONSORSHIPS

PAID SPONSORSHIPS AND REVIEWS

COMPANY / BUSINESS:

PRODUCT

CONTACT

OVERVIEW

KEYWORDS & LINKS

PUBLISH DATE   /   /   INCOME

NOTES   THOUGHTS/OVERVIEW

COMPANY / BUSINESS:

PRODUCT

CONTACT

OVERVIEW

KEYWORDS & LINKS

PUBLISH DATE   /   /   INCOME

NOTES   THOUGHTS/OVERVIEW

COMPANY / BUSINESS:

PRODUCT

CONTACT

OVERVIEW

KEYWORDS & LINKS

PUBLISH DATE   /   /   INCOME

NOTES   THOUGHTS/OVERVIEW

POST PLANNER

BLOG POST PLANNER

POST TITLE: _____   POSTING DATE: _____

TYPE/FORMAT: ARTICLE ☐   REVIEW ☐   TUTORIAL ☐   SPONSORED ☐   GUEST POST ☐

BLOG POST OVERVIEW/SUMMARY

BLOG POST IDEAS FOR THE MONTH

NEWSLETTER/MAILING LIST PROMO

OTHER PROMOTIONAL CHANNELS

MONTHLY REFLECTION

IDEAS TO GROW TRAFFIC NEXT MONTH

ADVERTISING & PROMOTION

TAGS & KEYWORDS

RESEARCH

SOURCES

CROSS POSTING & GUEST BLOGGING

SOCIAL MEDIA

FUTURE FOLLOW UP / CROSS MARKETING IDEAS

NEWSLETTER OUTREACH

NEWSLETTER TRACKER

NEWSLETTER TOPIC:	PUBLISHED:

CONTENT:

# SUBSCRIBERS:	OPEN RATES:	CTR:

NEWSLETTER TOPIC:	PUBLISHED:

CONTENT:

# SUBSCRIBERS:	OPEN RATES:	CTR:

NEWSLETTER TOPIC:	PUBLISHED:

CONTENT:

# SUBSCRIBERS:	OPEN RATES:	CTR:

NEWSLETTER TOPIC:	PUBLISHED:

CONTENT:

# SUBSCRIBERS:	OPEN RATES:	CTR:

FUTURE NEWSLETTER SUBJECT LINES & IDEAS

MARKETING

ADVERTISING IDEAS TO MAXIMIZE OUTREACH

SOCIAL MEDIA FOCUS:	MARKETING CHANNELS	ADVERTISING FOCUS
☐ ⓘ INSTAGRAM		
☐ 🐦 TWITTER		
☐ ⓟ PINTEREST		
☐ f FACEBOOK		
☐ ▶ YOUTUBE		
☐ 📺 TWITCH		
☐ 👻 SNAPCHAT		
☐ in LINKEDIN		
☐ Ⓑ BLOG		
☐		
☐		

MARKETING STRATEGY

CHANNEL

TARGET GOAL

MARKETING IDEAS

ACTION PLAN

LINKED IN POSTS

LINKEDIN POSTS & UPDATE PLANNER

POST

SUMMARY		PUBLISHED / /
		SPONSORED / PAID BY
		REMINDERS & TO DO
		☐
		☐
TAGS	HASHTAGS	☐
@	#	☐
@	#	☐
@	#	☐

POST

SUMMARY		PUBLISHED / /
		SPONSORED BY
		REMINDERS & TO DO
		☐
		☐
TAGS	HASHTAGS	☐
@	#	☐
@	#	☐
@	#	☐

POST

SUMMARY		PUBLISHED / /
		SPONSORED BY
		REMINDERS & TO DO
		☐
		☐
TAGS	HASHTAGS	☐
@	#	☐
@	#	☐
@	#	☐

INSTAGRAM POSTS

INSTAGRAM POSTS & UPDATE PLANNER

POST TITLE:

SUMMARY:		PUBLISHED ON: / /
		SPONSORED/PAID BY:
		REMINDERS & TO DO
		☐
TAGS		☐
LINKS	HASHTAGS	☐
@	#	☐
@	#	☐
@	#	☐

POST TITLE:

SUMMARY:		PUBLISHED ON: / /
		SPONSORED/PAID BY:
		REMINDERS & TO DO
		☐
TAGS		☐
LINKS	HASHTAGS	☐
@	#	☐
@	#	☐
@	#	☐

POST TITLE:

SUMMARY:		PUBLISHED ON: / /
		SPONSORED/PAID BY:
		REMINDERS & TO DO
		☐
TAGS		☐
LINKS	HASHTAGS	☐
@	#	☐
@	#	☐
@	#	☐

PINTEREST PLANNER

PINTEREST VISION BOARD AND PLANNER

BOARD #1	BOARD #2	BOARD #3	BOARD #4	BOARD #5

BOARD #6	BOARD #7	BOARD #8	BOARD #9	BOARD #10

Top Performing Pins

What's Currently Trending on Pinterest?

Most Popular Boards

Pins to Revive

Main Keywords

Included Elements

- ☐ BLOG POSTS
- ☐ SPONSORS
- ☐ ETSY
- ☐ TESTIMONIALS
- ☐ REVIEW
- ☐ SPOTLIGHT
- ☐
- ☐
- ☐
- ☐

Notes

PINTEREST PLANNER

PINTEREST MARKETING PLANNER

FOLLOWING

DAILY PIN GOAL

TOP PINS OF THE WEEK

TOP KEYWORDS OF THE WEEK

MONDAY	TUESDAY	WEDNESDAY	THURSDAY
KEYWORDS	KEYWORDS	KEYWORDS	KEYWORDS

FRIDAY	SATURDAY	SUNDAY	NOTES
KEYWORDS	KEYWORDS	KEYWORDS	KEYWORDS

FACEBOOK PLANNER

FACEBOOK MARKETING PLANNER

FOLLOWING

TARGET GOAL

SCHEDULED POSTS

TOP POSTS

MONDAY	TUESDAY	WEDNESDAY	THURSDAY
TRAFFIC STATS	TRAFFIC STATS	TRAFFIC STATS	TRAFFIC STATS

FRIDAY	SATURDAY	SUNDAY	NOTES
TRAFFIC STATS	TRAFFIC STATS	TRAFFIC STATS	TRAFFIC STATS

YOUTUBE UPDATES

SUMMARY OF UPDATE

☐ FILMED ☐ EDITED ☐ THUMBNAIL ☐ DESCRIPTION ☐ PUBLISHED

SUMMARY OF UPDATE

☐ FILMED ☐ EDITED ☐ THUMBNAIL ☐ DESCRIPTION ☐ PUBLISHED

SUMMARY OF UPDATE

☐ FILMED ☐ EDITED ☐ THUMBNAIL ☐ DESCRIPTION ☐ PUBLISHED

SUMMARY OF UPDATE

☐ FILMED ☐ EDITED ☐ THUMBNAIL ☐ DESCRIPTION ☐ PUBLISHED

SUMMARY OF UPDATE

☐ FILMED ☐ EDITED ☐ THUMBNAIL ☐ DESCRIPTION ☐ PUBLISHED

SUMMARY OF UPDATE

☐ FILMED ☐ EDITED ☐ THUMBNAIL ☐ DESCRIPTION ☐ PUBLISHED

SUMMARY OF UPDATE

☐ FILMED ☐ EDITED ☐ THUMBNAIL ☐ DESCRIPTION ☐ PUBLISHED

SPONSORED POSTS

PAID SPONSORSHIPS & POSTS

COMPANY	REVIEW	DEADLINE	EARNINGS	COMPLETED

HASHTAG IDEAS

HASHTAGS RESEARCH AND IDEAS

POST THEME:

Tag #1

Tag #2

Tag #3

Tag #4

Tag #5

Tag #6

Tag #7

Tag #8

POST THEME:

Tag #1

Tag #2

Tag #3

Tag #4

Tag #5

Tag #6

Tag #7

Tag #8

POST THEME:

Tag #1

Tag #2

Tag #3

Tag #4

Tag #5

Tag #6

Tag #7

Tag #8

POST THEME:

Tag #1

Tag #2

Tag #3

Tag #4

Tag #5

Tag #6

Tag #7

Tag #8

POST THEME:

Tag #1

Tag #2

Tag #3

Tag #4

Tag #5

Tag #6

Tag #7

Tag #8

POST THEME:

Tag #1

Tag #2

Tag #3

Tag #4

Tag #5

Tag #6

Tag #7

Tag #8

SOCIAL MEDIA

SOCIAL MEDIA UPDATE TRACKER

DATE ☐ CONTENT ☐ PHOTO / VIDEO

OTHER

DATE ☐ CONTENT ☐ PHOTO / VIDEO

OTHER

DATE ☐ CONTENT ☐ PHOTO / VIDEO

OTHER

DATE ☐ CONTENT ☐ PHOTO / VIDEO

OTHER

DATE ☐ CONTENT ☐ PHOTO / VIDEO

OTHER

DATA ANALYSIS

BUSINESS GROWTH, DATA CHARTS, PROGRESS

CHART FOR:

CHART FOR:

DAILY PLANNER

DATE: M T W T F S S

TODAY'S TO DO LIST	NOTES & MEMOS

BLOG POSTS & SOCIAL MEDIA UPDATES	IDEAS FOR FUTURE POSTS
☐	
☐	
☐	
☐	
☐	
☐	
☐	
☐	

DAILY PLANNER

DATE:

M T W T F S S

TODAY'S TO DO LIST

NOTES & MEMOS

BLOG POSTS & SOCIAL MEDIA UPDATES

IDEAS FOR FUTURE POSTS

DAILY PLANNER

DATE: _____   M T W T F S S

TODAY'S TO DO LIST	NOTES & MEMOS

BLOG POSTS & SOCIAL MEDIA UPDATES

- ☐
- ☐
- ☐
- ☐
- ☐
- ☐
- ☐
- ☐
- ☐

IDEAS FOR FUTURE POSTS

DAILY PLANNER

DATE: M T W T F S S

TODAY'S TO DO LIST

NOTES & MEMOS

BLOG POSTS & SOCIAL MEDIA UPDATES

☐
☐
☐
☐
☐
☐
☐
☐
☐

IDEAS FOR FUTURE POSTS

DAILY PLANNER

DATE: M T W T F S S

TODAY'S TO DO LIST

NOTES & MEMOS

BLOG POSTS & SOCIAL MEDIA UPDATES

IDEAS FOR FUTURE POSTS

DAILY PLANNER

DATE: M T W T F S S

TODAY'S TO DO LIST

NOTES & MEMOS

BLOG POSTS & SOCIAL MEDIA UPDATES

IDEAS FOR FUTURE POSTS

DAILY PLANNER

DATE: M T W T F S S

TODAY'S TO DO LIST

NOTES & MEMOS

BLOG POSTS & SOCIAL MEDIA UPDATES

- [ ]
- [ ]
- [ ]
- [ ]
- [ ]
- [ ]
- [ ]
- [ ]
- [ ]

IDEAS FOR FUTURE POSTS

DAILY PLANNER

DATE: M T W T F S S

TODAY'S TO DO LIST

NOTES & MEMOS

BLOG POSTS & SOCIAL MEDIA UPDATES

- [ ]
- [ ]
- [ ]
- [ ]
- [ ]
- [ ]
- [ ]
- [ ]
- [ ]

IDEAS FOR FUTURE POSTS

DAILY PLANNER

DATE: M T W T F S S

TODAY'S TO DO LIST

NOTES & MEMOS

BLOG POSTS & SOCIAL MEDIA UPDATES

IDEAS FOR FUTURE POSTS

DAILY PLANNER

DATE: M T W T F S S

TODAY'S TO DO LIST

NOTES & MEMOS

BLOG POSTS & SOCIAL MEDIA UPDATES

IDEAS FOR FUTURE POSTS

DAILY PLANNER

DATE: M T W T F S S

TODAY'S TO DO LIST	NOTES & MEMOS

BLOG POSTS & SOCIAL MEDIA UPDATES	IDEAS FOR FUTURE POSTS
☐	
☐	
☐	
☐	
☐	
☐	
☐	
☐	

DAILY PLANNER

TODAY'S TO DO LIST

NOTES & MEMOS

BLOG POSTS & SOCIAL MEDIA UPDATES

- [ ]
- [ ]
- [ ]
- [ ]
- [ ]
- [ ]
- [ ]
- [ ]
- [ ]

IDEAS FOR FUTURE POSTS

DAILY PLANNER

DATE: M T W T F S S

TODAY'S TO DO LIST

NOTES & MEMOS

BLOG POSTS & SOCIAL MEDIA UPDATES

IDEAS FOR FUTURE POSTS

DAILY PLANNER

DATE: M T W T F S S

TODAY'S TO DO LIST

NOTES & MEMOS

BLOG POSTS & SOCIAL MEDIA UPDATES

IDEAS FOR FUTURE POSTS

DAILY PLANNER

DATE:

TODAY'S TO DO LIST

NOTES & MEMOS

BLOG POSTS & SOCIAL MEDIA UPDATES

- [ ]
- [ ]
- [ ]
- [ ]
- [ ]
- [ ]
- [ ]
- [ ]
- [ ]

IDEAS FOR FUTURE POSTS

DAILY PLANNER

DATE:

TODAY'S TO DO LIST

NOTES & MEMOS

BLOG POSTS & SOCIAL MEDIA UPDATES

IDEAS FOR FUTURE POSTS

DAILY PLANNER

DATE: M T W T F S S

TODAY'S TO DO LIST

NOTES & MEMOS

BLOG POSTS & SOCIAL MEDIA UPDATES

- [ ]
- [ ]
- [ ]
- [ ]
- [ ]
- [ ]
- [ ]
- [ ]
- [ ]

IDEAS FOR FUTURE POSTS

DAILY PLANNER

DATE: M T W T F S S

TODAY'S TO DO LIST

NOTES & MEMOS

BLOG POSTS & SOCIAL MEDIA UPDATES

- [ ]
- [ ]
- [ ]
- [ ]
- [ ]
- [ ]
- [ ]
- [ ]
- [ ]

IDEAS FOR FUTURE POSTS

DAILY PLANNER

DATE: M T W T F S S

TODAY'S TO DO LIST	NOTES & MEMOS

BLOG POSTS & SOCIAL MEDIA UPDATES

- [ ]
- [ ]
- [ ]
- [ ]
- [ ]
- [ ]
- [ ]
- [ ]
- [ ]

IDEAS FOR FUTURE POSTS

DAILY PLANNER

DATE: M T W T F S S

TODAY'S TO DO LIST

NOTES & MEMOS

BLOG POSTS & SOCIAL MEDIA UPDATES

IDEAS FOR FUTURE POSTS

DAILY PLANNER

DATE: M T W T F S S

TODAY'S TO DO LIST

NOTES & MEMOS

BLOG POSTS & SOCIAL MEDIA UPDATES

IDEAS FOR FUTURE POSTS

DAILY PLANNER

DATE: M T W T F S S

TODAY'S TO DO LIST

NOTES & MEMOS

BLOG POSTS & SOCIAL MEDIA UPDATES

IDEAS FOR FUTURE POSTS

DAILY PLANNER

DATE: M T W T F S S

TODAY'S TO DO LIST	NOTES & MEMOS

BLOG POSTS & SOCIAL MEDIA UPDATES

☐
☐
☐
☐
☐
☐
☐
☐
☐

IDEAS FOR FUTURE POSTS

DAILY PLANNER

DATE: _____   M T W T F S S

TODAY'S TO DO LIST	NOTES & MEMOS

BLOG POSTS & SOCIAL MEDIA UPDATES

- [ ]
- [ ]
- [ ]
- [ ]
- [ ]
- [ ]
- [ ]
- [ ]
- [ ]

IDEAS FOR FUTURE POSTS

DAILY PLANNER

DATE: M T W T F S S

TODAY'S TO DO LIST

NOTES & MEMOS

BLOG POSTS & SOCIAL MEDIA UPDATES

IDEAS FOR FUTURE POSTS

DAILY PLANNER

DATE: M T W T F S S

TODAY'S TO DO LIST

NOTES & MEMOS

BLOG POSTS & SOCIAL MEDIA UPDATES

IDEAS FOR FUTURE POSTS

DAILY PLANNER

DATE: _____ M T W T F S S

TODAY'S TO DO LIST

NOTES & MEMOS

BLOG POSTS & SOCIAL MEDIA UPDATES

- [ ]
- [ ]
- [ ]
- [ ]
- [ ]
- [ ]
- [ ]
- [ ]
- [ ]

IDEAS FOR FUTURE POSTS

DAILY PLANNER

DATE: M T W T F S S

TODAY'S TO DO LIST

NOTES & MEMOS

BLOG POSTS & SOCIAL MEDIA UPDATES

- [ ]
- [ ]
- [ ]
- [ ]
- [ ]
- [ ]
- [ ]
- [ ]

IDEAS FOR FUTURE POSTS

DAILY PLANNER

DATE: M T W T F S S

TODAY'S TO DO LIST

NOTES & MEMOS

BLOG POSTS & SOCIAL MEDIA UPDATES

IDEAS FOR FUTURE POSTS

DAILY PLANNER

DATE: M T W T F S S

TODAY'S TO DO LIST

NOTES & MEMOS

BLOG POSTS & SOCIAL MEDIA UPDATES

IDEAS FOR FUTURE POSTS

DAILY PLANNER

DATE: M T W T F S S

TODAY'S TO DO LIST

NOTES & MEMOS

BLOG POSTS & SOCIAL MEDIA UPDATES

- [ ]
- [ ]
- [ ]
- [ ]
- [ ]
- [ ]
- [ ]
- [ ]
- [ ]

IDEAS FOR FUTURE POSTS

DAILY PLANNER

DATE:

TODAY'S TO DO LIST	NOTES & MEMOS

BLOG POSTS & SOCIAL MEDIA UPDATES

IDEAS FOR FUTURE POSTS

DAILY PLANNER

DATE: M T W T F S S

TODAY'S TO DO LIST

NOTES & MEMOS

BLOG POSTS & SOCIAL MEDIA UPDATES

- [ ]
- [ ]
- [ ]
- [ ]
- [ ]
- [ ]
- [ ]
- [ ]
- [ ]

IDEAS FOR FUTURE POSTS

DAILY PLANNER

DATE: M T W T F S S

TODAY'S TO DO LIST	NOTES & MEMOS

BLOG POSTS & SOCIAL MEDIA UPDATES	IDEAS FOR FUTURE POSTS
☐	
☐	
☐	
☐	
☐	
☐	
☐	
☐	

DAILY PLANNER

DATE: M T W T F S S

TODAY'S TO DO LIST	NOTES & MEMOS

BLOG POSTS & SOCIAL MEDIA UPDATES

- [ ]
- [ ]
- [ ]
- [ ]
- [ ]
- [ ]
- [ ]
- [ ]
- [ ]

IDEAS FOR FUTURE POSTS

DAILY PLANNER

DATE: M T W T F S S

TODAY'S TO DO LIST	NOTES & MEMOS

BLOG POSTS & SOCIAL MEDIA UPDATES

☐
☐
☐
☐
☐
☐
☐
☐
☐

IDEAS FOR FUTURE POSTS

DAILY PLANNER

DATE: \quad M T W T F S S

TODAY'S TO DO LIST

NOTES & MEMOS

BLOG POSTS & SOCIAL MEDIA UPDATES

- [ ]
- [ ]
- [ ]
- [ ]
- [ ]
- [ ]
- [ ]
- [ ]
- [ ]

IDEAS FOR FUTURE POSTS

DAILY PLANNER

DATE: M T W T F S S

TODAY'S TO DO LIST

NOTES & MEMOS

BLOG POSTS & SOCIAL MEDIA UPDATES

IDEAS FOR FUTURE POSTS

DAILY PLANNER

DATE: M T W T F S S

TODAY'S TO DO LIST

NOTES & MEMOS

BLOG POSTS & SOCIAL MEDIA UPDATES

IDEAS FOR FUTURE POSTS

DAILY PLANNER

DATE: M T W T F S S

TODAY'S TO DO LIST	NOTES & MEMOS

BLOG POSTS & SOCIAL MEDIA UPDATES

- [ ]
- [ ]
- [ ]
- [ ]
- [ ]
- [ ]
- [ ]
- [ ]
- [ ]

IDEAS FOR FUTURE POSTS

DAILY PLANNER

DATE: _____   M T W T F S S

TODAY'S TO DO LIST	NOTES & MEMOS

BLOG POSTS & SOCIAL MEDIA UPDATES

- [ ]
- [ ]
- [ ]
- [ ]
- [ ]
- [ ]
- [ ]
- [ ]
- [ ]

IDEAS FOR FUTURE POSTS

DAILY PLANNER

DATE: M T W T F S S

TODAY'S TO DO LIST

NOTES & MEMOS

BLOG POSTS & SOCIAL MEDIA UPDATES

IDEAS FOR FUTURE POSTS

DAILY PLANNER

DATE: M T W T F S S

TODAY'S TO DO LIST

NOTES & MEMOS

BLOG POSTS & SOCIAL MEDIA UPDATES

- [ ]
- [ ]
- [ ]
- [ ]
- [ ]
- [ ]
- [ ]
- [ ]
- [ ]

IDEAS FOR FUTURE POSTS

DAILY PLANNER

DATE: M T W T F S S

TODAY'S TO DO LIST

NOTES & MEMOS

BLOG POSTS & SOCIAL MEDIA UPDATES

- [ ]
- [ ]
- [ ]
- [ ]
- [ ]
- [ ]
- [ ]
- [ ]
- [ ]

IDEAS FOR FUTURE POSTS

DAILY PLANNER

DATE: M T W T F S S

TODAY'S TO DO LIST

NOTES & MEMOS

BLOG POSTS & SOCIAL MEDIA UPDATES

☐
☐
☐
☐
☐
☐
☐
☐
☐

IDEAS FOR FUTURE POSTS

DAILY PLANNER

DATE: M T W T F S S

TODAY'S TO DO LIST

NOTES & MEMOS

BLOG POSTS & SOCIAL MEDIA UPDATES

IDEAS FOR FUTURE POSTS

DAILY PLANNER

DATE: M T W T F S S

TODAY'S TO DO LIST

NOTES & MEMOS

BLOG POSTS & SOCIAL MEDIA UPDATES

☐
☐
☐
☐
☐
☐
☐
☐
☐

IDEAS FOR FUTURE POSTS

DAILY PLANNER

DATE: M T W T F S S

TODAY'S TO DO LIST

NOTES & MEMOS

BLOG POSTS & SOCIAL MEDIA UPDATES

- [ ]
- [ ]
- [ ]
- [ ]
- [ ]
- [ ]
- [ ]
- [ ]
- [ ]

IDEAS FOR FUTURE POSTS

DAILY PLANNER

DATE: M T W T F S S

TODAY'S TO DO LIST

NOTES & MEMOS

BLOG POSTS & SOCIAL MEDIA UPDATES

☐

☐

☐

☐

☐

☐

☐

☐

☐

IDEAS FOR FUTURE POSTS

DAILY PLANNER

DATE: M T W T F S S

TODAY'S TO DO LIST	NOTES & MEMOS

BLOG POSTS & SOCIAL MEDIA UPDATES

IDEAS FOR FUTURE POSTS

DAILY PLANNER

DATE: M T W T F S S

TODAY'S TO DO LIST	NOTES & MEMOS

BLOG POSTS & SOCIAL MEDIA UPDATES

☐
☐
☐
☐
☐
☐
☐
☐
☐

IDEAS FOR FUTURE POSTS

DAILY PLANNER

DATE: M T W T F S S

TODAY'S TO DO LIST

NOTES & MEMOS

BLOG POSTS & SOCIAL MEDIA UPDATES

- [ ]
- [ ]
- [ ]
- [ ]
- [ ]
- [ ]
- [ ]
- [ ]

IDEAS FOR FUTURE POSTS

DAILY PLANNER

DATE: M T W T F S S

TODAY'S TO DO LIST	NOTES & MEMOS

BLOG POSTS & SOCIAL MEDIA UPDATES	IDEAS FOR FUTURE POSTS
☐	
☐	
☐	
☐	
☐	
☐	
☐	
☐	

DAILY PLANNER

DATE: M T W T F S S

TODAY'S TO DO LIST	NOTES & MEMOS

BLOG POSTS & SOCIAL MEDIA UPDATES   IDEAS FOR FUTURE POSTS

DAILY PLANNER

DATE: M T W T F S S

TODAY'S TO DO LIST

NOTES & MEMOS

BLOG POSTS & SOCIAL MEDIA UPDATES

☐
☐
☐
☐
☐
☐
☐
☐
☐

IDEAS FOR FUTURE POSTS

DAILY PLANNER

DATE: M T W T F S S

TODAY'S TO DO LIST	NOTES & MEMOS

BLOG POSTS & SOCIAL MEDIA UPDATES

- [ ]
- [ ]
- [ ]
- [ ]
- [ ]
- [ ]
- [ ]
- [ ]

IDEAS FOR FUTURE POSTS

DAILY PLANNER

DATE: _____   M T W T F S S

TODAY'S TO DO LIST

NOTES & MEMOS

BLOG POSTS & SOCIAL MEDIA UPDATES

- [ ]
- [ ]
- [ ]
- [ ]
- [ ]
- [ ]
- [ ]
- [ ]
- [ ]

IDEAS FOR FUTURE POSTS

DAILY PLANNER

DATE: M T W T F S S

TODAY'S TO DO LIST

NOTES & MEMOS

BLOG POSTS & SOCIAL MEDIA UPDATES

- [ ]
- [ ]
- [ ]
- [ ]
- [ ]
- [ ]
- [ ]
- [ ]

IDEAS FOR FUTURE POSTS

DAILY PLANNER

DATE: M T W T F S S

TODAY'S TO DO LIST

NOTES & MEMOS

BLOG POSTS & SOCIAL MEDIA UPDATES

- [ ]
- [ ]
- [ ]
- [ ]
- [ ]
- [ ]
- [ ]
- [ ]
- [ ]

IDEAS FOR FUTURE POSTS

DAILY PLANNER

DATE: M T W T F S S

TODAY'S TO DO LIST

NOTES & MEMOS

BLOG POSTS & SOCIAL MEDIA UPDATES

- [ ]
- [ ]
- [ ]
- [ ]
- [ ]
- [ ]
- [ ]
- [ ]
- [ ]

IDEAS FOR FUTURE POSTS

DAILY PLANNER

DATE: M T W T F S S

TODAY'S TO DO LIST

NOTES & MEMOS

BLOG POSTS & SOCIAL MEDIA UPDATES

☐

☐

☐

☐

☐

☐

☐

☐

☐

IDEAS FOR FUTURE POSTS

DAILY PLANNER

DATE: M T W T F S S

TODAY'S TO DO LIST

NOTES & MEMOS

BLOG POSTS & SOCIAL MEDIA UPDATES

IDEAS FOR FUTURE POSTS

DAILY PLANNER

DATE: M T W T F S S

TODAY'S TO DO LIST

NOTES & MEMOS

BLOG POSTS & SOCIAL MEDIA UPDATES

- ☐
- ☐
- ☐
- ☐
- ☐
- ☐
- ☐
- ☐
- ☐

IDEAS FOR FUTURE POSTS

DAILY PLANNER

DATE: M T W T F S S

TODAY'S TO DO LIST

NOTES & MEMOS

BLOG POSTS & SOCIAL MEDIA UPDATES

☐
☐
☐
☐
☐
☐
☐
☐

IDEAS FOR FUTURE FOSTS

DAILY PLANNER

DATE: M T W T F S S

TODAY'S TO DO LIST	NOTES & MEMOS

BLOG POSTS & SOCIAL MEDIA UPDATES	IDEAS FOR FUTURE POSTS
☐	
☐	
☐	
☐	
☐	
☐	
☐	
☐	
☐	

DAILY PLANNER

DATE: M T W T F S S

TODAY'S TO DO LIST

NOTES & MEMOS

BLOG POSTS & SOCIAL MEDIA UPDATES

- [ ]
- [ ]
- [ ]
- [ ]
- [ ]
- [ ]
- [ ]
- [ ]
- [ ]

IDEAS FOR FUTURE POSTS

DAILY PLANNER

DATE: M T W T F S S

TODAY'S TO DO LIST

NOTES & MEMOS

BLOG POSTS & SOCIAL MEDIA UPDATES

- [ ]
- [ ]
- [ ]
- [ ]
- [ ]
- [ ]
- [ ]
- [ ]
- [ ]

IDEAS FOR FUTURE POSTS

DAILY PLANNER

DATE: M T W T F S S

TODAY'S TO DO LIST	NOTES & MEMOS

BLOG POSTS & SOCIAL MEDIA UPDATES

- [ ]
- [ ]
- [ ]
- [ ]
- [ ]
- [ ]
- [ ]
- [ ]
- [ ]

IDEAS FOR FUTURE POSTS

DAILY PLANNER

DATE: M T W T F S S

TODAY'S TO DO LIST

NOTES & MEMOS

BLOG POSTS & SOCIAL MEDIA UPDATES

- [ ]
- [ ]
- [ ]
- [ ]
- [ ]
- [ ]
- [ ]
- [ ]
- [ ]

IDEAS FOR FUTURE POSTS

DAILY PLANNER

DATE: M T W T F S S

TODAY'S TO DO LIST

NOTES & MEMOS

BLOG POSTS & SOCIAL MEDIA UPDATES

IDEAS FOR FUTURE POSTS

DAILY PLANNER

DATE: M T W T F S S

TODAY'S TO DO LIST

NOTES & MEMOS

BLOG POSTS & SOCIAL MEDIA UPDATES

- [ ]
- [ ]
- [ ]
- [ ]
- [ ]
- [ ]
- [ ]
- [ ]
- [ ]

IDEAS FOR FUTURE POSTS

DAILY PLANNER

DATE: M T W T F S S

TODAY'S TO DO LIST

NOTES & MEMOS

BLOG POSTS & SOCIAL MEDIA UPDATES

☐
☐
☐
☐
☐
☐
☐
☐

IDEAS FOR FUTURE POSTS

DAILY PLANNER

DATE: M T W T F S S

TODAY'S TO DO LIST

NOTES & MEMOS

BLOG POSTS & SOCIAL MEDIA UPDATES

IDEAS FOR FUTURE POSTS

Made in the USA
Las Vegas, NV
14 April 2022